To:

_____

From:

_____

——————— ———————

It's in Christ that we find out who we are and
what we are living for. Long before we first heard
of Christ... he had his eye on us, had designs
on us for glorious living, part of the overall purpose
he is working out in everything and everyone.
EPHESIANS 1:11 MSG

Requests for information should be addressed to:
Inspirio, the gift group of Zondervan
Grand Rapids, Michigan 49530
http://www.inspiriogifts.com

Compiler: Robin Schmitt
Editor: Janice Jacobson
Design Manager: Amy J. Wenger
Designer: Sherri L. Hoffman
Illustrator: Michael Halbert ©2002

Printed in the United States of America

04 05 06/ RRD/ 6 5 4

RICK WARREN

THE
PURPOSE
DRIVEN
Life
Prayer Journal

A companion to
The Purpose-Driven® Life

ψ
inspirio™

A JOURNEY WITH PURPOSE

Before you were born, God planned this moment in your life. It is no accident that you have chosen to read The Purpose-Driven Life. God longs for you to discover the life he created you to live—here on earth, and forever in eternity.

As I wrote Purpose-Driven Life, I prayed you would experience the incredible joy that comes from knowing God's purposes for your life. I admire you for your interest in this book. It shows you want to know your purpose, and God loves that. You'll learn the big picture—how all the pieces of the puzzle fit together. This perspective on life will reduce your stress, increase your satisfaction, help you make better decisions, and most importantly, prepare you for eternity.

I invite you to join me in a life-defining *40-day spiritual journey* that answers life's most important question: What on earth am I here for? The best way to reinforce your progress in fulfilling God's purposes for your life is to keep a spiritual journal. This is not a diary of events, but a record of the life lessons you don't want to forget. We remember what we record. Writing helps clarify what God is doing in your life.

If you're serious about fulfilling your life's purpose you can't be in a hurry. God isn't. So slow down and take the time to reflect, discuss what you read each day, and then journal. Allow the Scripture to speak to you.

Your life is a journey and a journey deserves a journal. You owe it to future generations to preserve the testimony of how God helped you to fulfill his purposes on earth. It is a witness that will continue long after you are in heaven.

— Rick Warren

Write down for the coming generation
what the LORD has done,
So that people not yet born will praise him.
PSALM 102:18 GNT

WHAT ON EARTH AM I HERE FOR?

day

IT ALL STARTS WITH GOD

For everything, absolutely everything, above and
below, visible and invisible, ... everything got started
in him and finds its purpose in him.
COLOSSIANS 1:16 MSG

POINT TO PONDER: It's not about me.

QUESTION TO CONSIDER: How can I remind myself today that life is really about living for God, not myself?

The purpose of your life is far greater than your own personal fulfillment, your peace of mind, or even your happiness. It's far greater than your family, your career, or even your wildest dreams and ambitions.

There is an alternative to speculation about the meaning and purpose of life. It's *revelation*. We can turn to what God has revealed about life in his Word. The easiest way to discover the purpose of an invention is to ask the creator of it. The same is true for discovering your life's purpose: ask God.

———————— ✍ ————————

God's wisdom ... goes deep into the interior of his purposes.
It's not the latest message, but more like the oldest—what
God determined as the way to bring out his best in us.
1 CORINTHIANS 2:7 MSG

_____

_____

_____

_____

_____

_____

_____

_____

_____

_____

_____

_____

_____

Father,

As I begin this journey, help me to realize that building my life
around myself instead of you will only lead to emptiness and
meaninglessness. I was made by you and for you, and I want to
discover my purpose in you.

day 2

YOU ARE NOT AN ACCIDENT

"I am your Creator. You were in my care even before you were born," says the LORD.
ISAIAH 44:2 CEV

POINT TO PONDER: I am not an accident.

QUESTION TO CONSIDER: Knowing that God created me for a purpose, what areas of my personality, background, and appearance do I need to accept?

Long before you were conceived by your parents you were conceived in the mind of God. It is not fate, nor chance, nor luck, nor coincidence that you are breathing at this very moment. You are alive because God wanted to create you!

_____

_____

_____

_____

_____

_____

_____

_____

_____

_____

O LORD, You saw me before I was born and scheduled each day of my life before I began to breathe. Every day was recorded in your book!
PSALM 139:16 LB

God made you to love you and you are his special creation.

God was thinking of you even *before* he made the world! In fact, that's why he created it! God designed this planet's environment just so we could live in it. We are the focus of his love, and the most valuable of all his creation.

_____

_____

_____

_____

_____

_____

_____

_____

_____

_____

_____

_____

_____

_____

_____

_____

_____

_____

Long before he laid down earth's foundations, he had us
in mind, had settled on us as the focus of his love.
EPHESIANS 1:4 MSG

If there was no God, then we'd all be "accidents," the result of astronomical random chance in the universe. But there *is* a God, he made you for a reason, and your life has profound meaning! We discover that meaning and purpose *only* when we make God the reference point of our lives.

_____

_____

_____

_____

_____

_____

_____

_____

_____

_____

> God doesn't play
> dice.
> ALBERT EINSTEIN

_____

_____

_____

_____

_____

_____

_____

_____

_____

God, your plan is amazing. Thank you that I was custom-made
for a reason. Help me to trust your wisdom in choosing my
parents, race, background, gifts, and appearance.

WHAT DRIVES YOUR LIFE?

━━━━━━━ ✺ ━━━━━━━

You, LORD, give perfect peace to those who keep their
purpose firm and put their trust in you.
ISAIAH 26:3 TEV

POINT TO PONDER: Living on purpose is the path to peace.

QUESTION TO CONSIDER: What would my family and friends say is
the driving force of my life? What do I want it to be?

Everyone's life is driven by something. Most dictionaries define the verb
drive as "to guide, to control, or to direct." Whether you are driving a car, a
nail, or a golf ball, you are guiding, controlling, and directing it at that
moment. What is the driving force in your life?

_____

_____

_____

_____

_____

_____

_____

_____

_____

_____

_____

_____

_____

_____

━━━━━━━ ✺ ━━━━━━━

Jesus said, "No one can serve two masters."
MATTHEW 6:24 NLT

Many people are driven by guilt, resentment and anger, fear, materialism, or the expectations of others. This journal will help you to live a *purpose driven* life—guided, controlled and directed by God's purposes. Nothing matters more than knowing God's purposes for your life.

We are all products of our past but we don't have to be prisoners of it. God's purpose is not limited by your past. He can turn a murderer (Moses) into a leader, a coward (Gideon) into a courageous hero, and he can do amazing things with the rest of your life.

_____

_____

_____

_____

_____

_____

_____

_____

_____

_____

_____

_____

_____

_____

_____

_____

_____

_____

There are five great benefits of living a purpose-driven life:

- Knowing your purpose gives your life meaning.
- Knowing your purpose simplifies your life.
- Knowing your purpose focuses your life.
- Knowing your purpose motivates your life, and ...

_____

_____

_____

_____

_____

_____

_____

_____

_____

_____

_____

_____

_____

_____

_____

_____

_____

_____

_____

• Fulfilling your purpose will create an eternal legacy.

Everyone wants to be remembered when they're gone. Ultimately, what matters most will not be what others say about your life but what *God* says about you. How will you answer God when he asks, *"What did you do with my Son, Jesus Christ?"* and *"What did you do with what I gave you?"*

_____

_____

_____

_____

_____   Remember, each of us
                                                 will stand personally
_____   before the judgment seat
                                                 of God. Yes, each of us
_____   will have to give a
                                                 personal account to God.
_____   **ROMANS 14:10, 12 NLT**

_____

_____

_____

_____

_____

_____

_____

_____

Father, I don't want my life to be driven by anything but love for you. Help me to center my life on your plan and purpose for me, and not worry about the expectations of others.

MADE TO LAST FOREVER

This world is fading away, along with everything it craves.
But if you do the will of God, you will live forever.
1 JOHN 2:17 NLT

POINT TO PONDER: There is more to life than just here and now.

QUESTION TO CONSIDER: Since everything has eternal consequences, what is one thing I should stop doing and one thing I should start doing today?

You have an inborn instinct that longs for immortality. This is because God designed you, in his image, to live for eternity. The reason we feel we should live forever is because God wired our brains with that desire! God has planted eternity in the human heart (Ecclesiastes 3:11 NLT).

> Surely God would not have created such a being as man to exist only for a day! No, no, man was made for immortality.
>
> ABRAHAM LINCOLN

How you relate to God now on earth will determine where you spend eternity. If you develop a relationship of love and trust in God through his Son Jesus Christ you'll spend the rest of eternity with him. When you live in light of eternity, your values change. You use your time and money more wisely. You place a higher premium on relationships and character instead of fame or wealth or achievements, or even fun. Your priorities are reordered. Keeping up with trends, fashions, and popular values, just doesn't matter as much anymore.

_____

_____

_____

_____

_____

_____

_____

_____

_____

_____

_____

_____

_____

_____

_____

_____

_____

_____

Paul wrote, "I once thought all these things were
so very important, but now I consider them
worthless because of what Christ has done."
PHILIPPIANS 3:7 NLT

--- ✍ ---

God's plans endure forever; his purposes last eternally.
PSALM 33:11 TEV

God has a purpose for your life on earth but it doesn't end here. His plan involves far more than the few decades you'll spend on this planet. It's more than "the opportunity of a lifetime"; God offers you an opportunity *beyond* your lifetime.

_____

_____

_____

_____

_____

_____

_____

_____

_____

_____

_____

_____

_____

_____

*God, open my eyes to see that there are eternal consequences
in even the smallest choices of my life. Remind me to look past
what is temporary and focus on what will last forever. Teach me
to live in light of eternity.*

SEEING LIFE FROM GOD'S VIEW

Unless you are faithful in small matters,
you won't be faithful in large ones.
LUKE 16:10 NLT

POINT TO PONDER: Life is a test and a trust.

QUESTION TO CONSIDER: What has happened to me recently that I now realize was a test from God? What are the greatest trusts God has entrusted to me?

The Bible says life is a test, life is a trust, and life is a temporary assignment. These ideas are the foundation of purpose driven living. To fulfill the purposes God created you for, you'll have to challenge conventional wisdom and replace it with the biblical metaphors of life.

_____

_____

_____

_____

_____

_____

_____

_____

_____

_____

Do not conform yourselves to the standards of this world,
but let God transform you inwardly by a complete change of
your mind. Then you will be able to know the will of God.
ROMANS 12:2 TEV.

When you understand that life is a test, you realize that *nothing* is insignificant in your life. Even the smallest incident has significance for your character. *Every* day is an important day, and every second is a growth opportunity to develop character, to demonstrate love, or to depend on God. Some tests seem enormous and overwhelming while others you don't even notice. But all of them have eternal implications.

_____

_____

_____

_____

_____

_____

_____

_____

_____

_____

_____

_____

_____

_____

_____

_____

_____

_____

——————— ✒ ———————

Blessed are those who endure when they are tested.
When they pass the test, they will receive the crown of life
that God has promised to those who love him.
JAMES 1:12 GWT

Never forget that everything in your life really belongs to God: your home, children, job—everything. You're just a caretaker, a trustee, a steward of it all. It's your privilege to enjoy it but it's also your responsibility to faithfully use it the way God wants it used.

Our culture says, "If you don't own it, you won't take care of it." But Christians live by a higher standard: "Because *God* owns it, I must take the best care of it that I can."

_____

_____

_____

_____

_____   Those who are trusted
                                                            with something valuable
_____   must show they are
                                                            worthy of that trust.
_____   **1 CORINTHIANS 4:2** NCV

_____

_____

_____

_____

_____

_____

_____

_____

_____

_____

_____

At the end of your life on earth you'll be evaluated and rewarded according to how well you handled what God entrusted to you. That means *everything* you do, even simple daily chores, has eternal implications. If you treat everything as a *trust*, God promises three rewards in eternity. First, you'll be given God's *affirmation:* He'll say, "Good job! Well done!" Next, you'll receive a *promotion* and be given greater responsibility in eternity: "I will put you in charge of many things." Then, you'll be honored with a *celebration:* "Come and share your Master's happiness."

_____

_____

_____

_____

_____

_____

_____

_____

_____

_____

_____

_____

_____

_____

_____

Gracious God, give me the wisdom to see life as you see it.
Help me to pass the test of character you place before me and
to treat everything you give me as a sacred trust. You own it all;
I just get to use it while I'm on earth.

LIFE IS A TEMPORARY ASSIGNMENT

We fix our eyes not on what is seen, but on what is unseen.
For what is seen is temporary, but what is unseen is eternal.
2 CORINTHIANS 4:18 NIV

POINT TO PONDER: This world is not my home

QUESTION TO CONSIDER: Since life on earth is just a temporary assignment, how should that change the way I live today?

To make the best use of your life you must never forget two truths: First, compared to eternity, life is brief. Second, earth is only a temporary residence for you. You won't be here long, so don't get too attached. Ask God to help you see life on earth as he sees it. With all the fascinating attractions, mesmerizing media, and enjoyable experiences available today, it's easy to forget that the pursuit of happiness is not what life is about. Only as we remember that life is a test, a trust, and a temporary assignment will the appeal of these things lose their grip on our lives.

_____

_____

_____

_____

_____

_____

_____

_____

The things we see now are here today, gone tomorrow.
But the things we can't see now will last forever.
2 CORINTHIANS 4:18 MSG

LIFE IS A TEMPORARY ASSIGNMENT

In God's eyes, the greatest heroes of faith are not those who achieve prosperity, success, and power in this life, but those who treat this life as a temporary assignment and serve faithfully expecting their promised reward in eternity.

_____

_____

_____

_____

_____

_____

_____

_____

_____

_____

_____

_____

_____

_____

_____

_____

_____

_____

_____

_____

_____

_____

"This world is fading away, along with everything it craves. But if you do the will of God, you will live forever."

1 JOHN 2:17 NLT

———— ✍ ————

We fix our eyes not on what is seen, but on what is unseen. For
what is seen is temporary, but what is unseen is eternal.
2 CORINTHIANS 4:18 NIV

When life gets tough, when you're overwhelmed with doubt, when you see
evil prospering, or when you wonder if living for Christ is worth the effort,
remember that you are not home yet. At death you won't leave home—
you'll *go* home.

_____

_____

_____

_____

_____

_____

_____

_____

_____

_____

_____

_____

_____

_____

*Lord, help me remember that there is more to life than
just here and now. Remind me to live like a temporary resident,
not getting too attached to the things of this world because
they are not what is going to last.*

day

THE REASON FOR EVERYTHING

— ❧ —

For everything comes from God alone. Everything lives
by his power, and everything is for his glory.
ROMANS 11:36 LB

POINT TO PONDER: It's all for Him.

QUESTION TO CONSIDER: How in my daily routine could I become
more aware of God's glory around me?

The ultimate goal of the universe is to show the glory of God. It is the
reason for everything that exists, including you. God made it *all* for his
glory. Living for God's glory is the greatest achievement you can accomplish
with your life. God says, *"They are my own people, and I created them to bring
me glory"* (Isaiah 43:7 TEV), so it ought to be the supreme goal of our lives.

_____

_____

_____

_____

_____

_____

_____

_____

_____

_____

_____

_____

Jesus honored God by fulfilling his purpose on earth. We bring God glory the same way.

There are many ways to bring glory to God but they can be summarized in God's five purposes for your life.

We bring God glory by worshiping him.
We bring God glory by loving other believers.
We bring God glory by becoming like Christ.
We bring God glory by serving others with our gifts.
We bring God glory by telling others about him.

There are three secrets about the glory of God that most people miss. First, when you trust Christ with your life, God puts his glory *in you!* The second secret is that the more you focus on living for God's glory, the more you will be filled with joy! The third secret is that if you've committed your life to Jesus, one day you are going to share in God's glory! God repeatedly promises that if we live for his glory on earth, we'll share his glory for eternity!

Will you live for your own goals, comfort, and pleasure, or will you live the rest of your life for God's glory, knowing that he's promised eternal rewards? You may hesitate, wondering if you'll have strength to live for God. Don't worry. Jesus will give you everything you need to live for him if you'll just make the choice to do it.

———————— ✍ ————————

Everything that goes into a life of pleasing God has been miraculously given to us by getting to know, personally and intimately, the One who invited us to God.
2 PETER 1:3 MSG

_____

_____

_____

_____

_____

_____

_____

_____

_____

_____

_____

_____

_____

_____

_____

Wonderful God, it is my deepest desire to bring you glory.
Help me to see your glory all around me today. Nothing would
exist without you. It's all for your glory!

purpose #

1

YOU WERE PLANNED
FOR GOD'S PLEASURE

day 8

PLANNED FOR GOD'S PLEASURE

The LORD takes pleasure in his people.
PSALM 149:4 TEV

POINT TO PONDER: I was planned for God's pleasure.

QUESTION TO CONSIDER: What could I start doing today as if I was doing it for Jesus?

Bringing pleasure to God is called worship. It is the first and primary purpose of your life. Anything you do that brings pleasure to God is an act of worship. Like a diamond, worship is *multifaceted*. Worship is a lifestyle.

_____

_____

_____

_____

_____

_____

_____

_____

_____

_____

_____

O Lord, you created everything, and it is for your pleasure
that they exist and were created.
REVELATION 4:11 NLT

We worship for God's benefit. When we worship, our goal is to bring
pleasure to God, not ourselves. Worship isn't for you. It's for God. Of
course, there are many benefits to worship, but we don't worship to please
ourselves. Our motive is to bring glory and pleasure to our Creator.

_____

_____

_____

_____

_____

_____

_____

_____

_____

_____

_____

_____

_____

_____

_____

_____

_____

_____

_____

_____

The LORD is pleased with those who
worship him and trust his love.

PSALM 147:11 CEV

⸺ ✍ ⸺

"Take your everyday, ordinary life—your sleeping, eating, going-to-work, and walking around life—and place it before God as an offering."

ROMANS 12:1 MSG

Worship is not what you do with your lips; it's what you do with your *life*. All the singing, praying, and praising is worthless if it doesn't lead to personal change and commitment. You can't be a spectator in worship. Passive worship is an oxymoron. Real worship is offering yourself to live for God's pleasure.

_____

_____

_____

_____

_____

_____

_____

_____

_____

_____

_____

_____

Father, thank you for creating me for your own pleasure!
I would not even exist if you hadn't chosen to make me. If I
don't get anything else done today, help me to know and love
you a little bit more before I go to sleep tonight. Help me
to develop a lifestyle of worship.

WHAT MAKES GOD SMILE?

The LORD is pleased with those who
worship him and trust his love.
PSALM 147:11 CEV

POINT TO PONDER: God smiles when I trust Him.

QUESTION TO CONSIDER: Since God knows what's best, in what areas
of my life do I need to trust him more?

Since bringing pleasure to God is the first purpose of your life, your most
important task is to discover how to do that. Fortunately, the Bible gives us
a clear example of a life that gives pleasure to God. The man's name was
Noah. From his life, we learn the five acts of worship that make God smile.

> God smiles when we love him supremely.
> God smiles when we trust him completely.
> God smiles when we obey him wholeheartedly.
> God smiles when we praise and thank him.
> God smiles when we fulfill his purposes.

This is what God wants most from you: a relationship! God deeply loves you and *desires* your love in return. He *longs* for you to know him and spend time with him. He delights in you. Building a relationship with God, and learning to love and be loved by him, should be the greatest objective of your life. Nothing else even comes close in importance.

_____

_____

_____

_____

_____

_____

_____

_____

_____

_____

_____

_____

_____

_____

_____

_____

_____

_____

_____

Jesus said, "Love the Lord your God with all your heart
and with all your soul and with all your mind. This is the
first and greatest commandment."
MATTHEW 22:37–38 NIV

We please God by what we do and
not only by what we believe.
JAMES 2:24 CEV

God's Word is very clear that you can't earn your salvation. It is only by grace, not your effort. But as a child of God you can bring pleasure to your heavenly Father through obedience. Search through your Bible and make a list of the small obediences that God says bring him pleasure. All of these can be acts of worship. Why is obedience so pleasing to God? Because it proves you really love him.

_____

_____

_____

_____

_____

_____

_____

_____

_____

_____

_____

_____

_____

_____

_____

_____

_____

Jesus said, "If you love me, you will obey my commandments."
JOHN 14:15 TEV

WHAT MAKES GOD SMILE?

The LORD looks down from heaven on all mankind to see if there are any who are wise, who want to please God.
PSALM 14:2 LB

When you live in light of eternity, the question changes from "How much pleasure am I getting out of life?" to "How much pleasure is God getting out of my life?" God is looking for people like Noah in the 21st century—people willing to live for the pleasure of God. This lifestyle of worship is the only wise, sensible way to live.

_____

_____

_____

_____

_____   *Figure out what*

_____   *will please Christ,*

_____   *and then do it.*
                                               EPHESIANS 5:10 MSG

_____

_____

_____

_____

_____

_____

_____

_____

Dear God, I want my life to bring a smile to your face.
Empower me to love you supremely, trust you completely
and obey you wholeheartedly today.

THE HEART OF WORSHIP

*Give yourselves to God . . . surrender your whole being
to him to be used for righteous purposes.*
ROMANS 6:13 TEV

POINT TO PONDER: The heart of worship is surrender.

QUESTION TO CONSIDER: What area of my life am I holding back
from God? What am I afraid of?

Surrendering to God is the heart of worship. True worship—bringing God
pleasure—happens when you give yourself completely to God. Offering
yourself to God is what worship is all about. This act of personal surrender is
called many things: consecration, making Jesus Lord, taking up your cross,
dying to self, yielding to the Spirit. What matters is that you do it, not what
you call it. God wants your life. All of it. 95% is not enough.

_____

_____

_____

_____

_____

_____

_____

_____

_____

_____

_____

_____

_____

_____

Trust is an essential ingredient to surrender. You won't surrender to God unless you trust him, but you can't trust him until you know him better. Fear keeps us from surrendering but *love casts out all fear.* The more you realize how much God loves you, the easier surrender becomes. God is a Lover and a Liberator, and surrendering brings freedom, not bondage. When we completely surrender ourselves to Jesus, we discover that he is not a tyrant but a Savior; not a boss, but a brother; not a dictator, but a friend.

Surrendering is best demonstrated in obedience; cooperating with your Creator. You say, *"Yes Lord"* to whatever he asks of you. The supreme example of self-surrender is Jesus. The night before his crucifixion Jesus surrendered himself to God's plan. He prayed, *"Father, everything is possible for you. Please take this cup of suffering away from me. Yet I want your will, not mine"* (Mark 14:36 NLT). Genuine surrender says, "Father, if this problem, pain, sickness, or circumstance is needed to fulfill your purpose and glory in my life or in another's, please *don't* take it away!"

_____

_____

_____

_____

_____

_____

_____

_____

_____

_____

_____

_____

_____

_____

_____

_____

_____

_____

_____

_____

Give yourselves completely to God.
JAMES 4:7 NCV

If God is going to do his deepest work in you, it will begin with surrender.
So give it all to God; your past regrets, your present problems, your future
ambitions, your fears, dreams, weaknesses, habits, hurts, and hang-ups. Put
Christ in the driver's seat of your life and take your hands off the steering
wheel. Don't be afraid; nothing under his control can ever be out of
control. Mastered by Christ, you can handle anything.

_____

_____

_____

_____

_____

_____
The heart of
worship is
surrender.

_____

_____

_____

_____

_____

_____

_____

Dear loving Father, when I think of all you've done for me, I want
to surrender all my life to your will. I want to give up my need to
control things and trust in you instead. Help me to hold back
nothing from you today.

BECOMING BEST FRIENDS WITH GOD

Friendship with God is reserved for those who reverence him.
PSALM 25:14 LB

POINT TO PONDER: God wants to be my best friend.

QUESTION TO CONSIDER: How could I remind myself to talk to God more often throughout my day?

Adam and Eve enjoyed an intimate friendship with God. Unhindered by guilt or fear, they delighted in God and he delighted in them. We were made to live in the environment of God's continual presence, but after the Fall that ideal relationship was lost. Yet because Jesus secured our salvation and left his Holy Spirit in us, we all can become friends of God now. *Since we were restored to friendship with God by the death of his Son while we were still his enemies, we will certainly be delivered from eternal punishment by his life* (Romans 5:10 NLT).

Now we can rejoice in our wonderful new relationship
with God—all because of what our Lord Jesus Christ has
done for us in making us friends of God.
ROMANS 5:11 NLT

BECOMING BEST FRIENDS WITH GOD

Friendship with God is built by sharing *all* your life experiences with him. God wants to be more than an appointment in your schedule. He wants to be included in *every* activity, every conversation, every problem, and even every thought. Friendships are built on shared experiences—celebrations, tragedies, challenges, routines, highs and lows. You build a friendship with God the same way: by spending time together interacting, talking, listening, and going through a variety of circumstances together.

_____

_____

_____

_____

_____

_____

_____

_____

_____

_____

_____

_____

_____

_____

_____

_____

It's impossible to be God's friend apart from *knowing what he says*. You can't love God unless you know him, and you can't know him without knowing his Word. While you cannot spend all day studying the Bible, you can *think* about it throughout the day, recalling verses you've read or memorized, and mulling them over in your mind. The reason God considered Job and David close friends was because they valued and esteemed his Word above everything else, and they thought about it continually throughout the day.

_____

_____

_____

_____

_____

_____

_____

_____

_____

_____

_____

_____

_____

_____

_____

_____

_____

Oh, LORD, how I love your law! I meditate on it all day long.
PSALM 119:97 NIV

BECOMING BEST FRIENDS WITH GOD

A third way to build a friendship with God is by being honest with him. God expects honesty, not perfection. If perfection was a requirement, none of us could ever be friends of God. None of God's friends in the Bible were perfect. We're only his friends by grace. Jesus is still the *"friend of sinners"* (Matthew 11:19). In the Bible, the friends of God were honest about their feelings. God, however, didn't seem to be bothered by this frankness; in fact, he encouraged it.

_____

_____

_____

_____

_____

_____   Knowing and loving

_____   God is our greatest

_____   privilege, and being

_____   known and loved is

_____   God's greatest

_____   pleasure.

_____

_____

_____

_____

_____

_____

_____

*Jesus, forgive me for being too busy to develop a friendship
with you. I want to develop a running dialogue, a continual
conversation with you throughout the day.*

DEVELOPING YOUR FRIENDSHIP WITH GOD

Draw close to God, and God will draw close to you.
JAMES 4:8 NLT

POINT TO PONDER: I'm as close to God as I choose to be

QUESTION TO CONSIDER: What choices will I make today in order to grow closer to God?

To instruct us in candid honesty, God gave us the book of Psalms—a worship manual, full of ranting, raving, doubts, fears, resentments, and deep passions combined with thanksgiving, praise, and statements of faith. Every possible emotion is catalogued in the Psalms. When you read the emotional confessions of David and others, realize this is how God wants you to worship him—holding back nothing of what you feel.

_____

_____

_____

_____

_____

_____

_____

_____

_____

_____

_____

_____

He offers his friendship to the godly.
PROVERBS 3:32 NLT

DEVELOPING YOUR FRIENDSHIP WITH GOD

You build a friendship with God by caring about what God cares about. This is what friends do—they care about what is important to the other person. The more you become God's friend, the more you will care about the things God cares about, grieve over the things God grieves over, and rejoice over the things that bring pleasure to God. What does God care about most? He wants all his lost children found! That's the whole reason Jesus came to earth. The dearest thing to the heart of God is the death of his Son. The second dearest thing is when his children share that news with others.

_____

_____

_____

_____

_____

_____

_____

_____

_____

_____

_____

_____

_____

_____

_____

_____

——————— ✒ ———————

O LORD, your love means more than life to me.
PSALM 63:3 CEV

You build a friendship with God by desiring it more than anything else. Intimate friendship with God is a choice, not an accident. You must intentionally seek it. Do you really want it—more than anything? You may have been passionate about God in the past but you've lost that desire. To re-ignite your passion for God, start asking God to give it to you, and keep on asking until you have it. Pray this throughout your day:

Dear Jesus, more than anything else, I want to get to know you intimately.

_____

_____

_____

_____

_____

_____

_____

_____

_____

_____

_____

_____

_____

_____

_____

_____

_____

_____

Jesus, I want a deeper relationship with you. Help me
to be completely honest with my feelings and my faults.
Nothing matters more than my relationship to you.

WORSHIP THAT PLEASES GOD

❧

Love the Lord your God with all your heart and with all your soul
and with all your mind and with all your strength.
MARK 12:30 NIV

POINT TO PONDER: God wants *all* of me.

QUESTION TO CONSIDER: Which is more pleasing to God right now –
my public worship or my private worship?   What will I do about this?

God-pleasing worship is based on Scripture. Real worship is rooted in the
Word; it's based on truth, not our imagination. God-pleasing worship is also
from the heart. Made in God's image, you are a spirit that resides in a body,
and God designed your spirit to communicate with him. Worship is our
spirit responding to God's Spirit.

_____

_____

_____

_____

_____

_____

_____

_____

_____

_____

_____

_____

❧

Let us be grateful and worship God in a way that
will please him, with reverence and awe.
HEBREWS 12:28 TEV

God-pleasing worship is thoughtful. Reading Scripture in different translations and paraphrases will expand your expressions of worship. Try praising God without using the words *praise, hallelujah, thanks,* or *amen.* Make a list of synonyms and use fresh words like *admire, respect, value, revere, honor, and appreciate.* Be *specific.* You'd rather receive two specific compliments than 20 vague generalities. So would God. Another idea is to make a list of the different names of God and focus on them. God's names are not arbitrary; they tell us about different aspects of his character. And God commands us to praise his name.

_____

_____

_____

_____

_____

_____

_____

_____

_____

_____

_____

_____

_____

_____

_____

_____

_____

_____

_____

_____

_____

_____

God-pleasing worship is sacrificial. Real worship costs. One thing worship costs us is our self-centeredness. You cannot exalt God and yourself at the same time. You don't worship to be seen by others or to please yourself. You deliberately shift the focus off yourself. When Jesus said, *"Love God with all your strength"* he pointed out that worship takes effort and energy. It is not always convenient or comfortable, and sometimes worship is a sheer act of the will—a willing sacrifice.

I will not offer to the LORD my God sacrifices
that have cost me nothing.
2 SAMUEL 24:24 TEV

--- ✍ ---

Praise him from sunrise to sunset.
PSALM 113:3 LB

God-pleasing worship is continual. Praise should be the first activity when you open your eyes in the morning and when you close them at night. Worship is not a part of your life, it *is* your life, and every activity can be transformed into an act of worship when you do it for the praise, glory, and pleasure of God.

_____

_____

_____

_____

--- ✍ ---

Worship is the first purpose of your life. It is our greatest responsibility, our highest privilege, and it should take priority over everything else.

--- ✍ ---

_____

_____

_____

_____

_____

_____

_____

_____

_____

*Father, I want to bring you pleasure today by loving you
with all my heart and mind and soul and strength. Help me
to identify and develop the sacred pathway that fits
how you created me to know you.*

WHEN GOD SEEMS DISTANT

God said, "I will never leave you; I will never abandon you."
HEBREWS 13:5 TEV

POINT TO PONDER: God is real, no matter how I feel

QUESTION TO CONSIDER: How do I intend to stay focused on God even when He feels distant?

Friendships are often tested by separation and silence. In your friendship with God, you won't always *feel* close to him. The deepest level of worship is praising God in spite of pain, thanking God during a trial, trusting God when tempted, surrendering while suffering, and loving God when he seems distant.

_____

_____

_____

_____

_____

_____

_____

_____

_____

_____

_____

_____

_____

_____

Any relationship involves times of closeness and times of distance, and in a relationship with God, no matter how intimate, the pendulum will swing from one side to the other.

PHILIP YANCEY

God has promised repeatedly, "I will *never* leave you nor forsake you" (Hebrews 13:5). But God has *not* promised, "You will always *feel* my presence." In fact, God admits that sometimes he hides his face from us. There will be times when God appears to be *MIA*, missing-in-action, in your life. It's a normal part of the testing and maturing of your friendship with God. *Every* single Christian goes through it at least once, and usually several times. It's painful and disconcerting, but it is absolutely vital for the development of your faith.

_____

_____

_____

_____

_____

_____

_____

_____

_____

_____

_____

——— *ॐ* ———

Faith develops
when you don't feel
anything.

——— *ॐ* ———

_____

_____

_____

_____

_____

_____

_____

God's omnipresence and the manifestation of his presence are two different things. One is a fact; the other is often a feeling. God is always present, even when you're unaware of him, and his presence is too profound to be measured by mere emotion. Yes, he wants you to sense his presence, but he's more concerned that you *trust* him than that you *feel* him. Faith, not feelings, pleases God.

———— ✍ ————

Naked I came from my mother's womb, and naked
I will depart. The LORD gave and the LORD has taken away;
may the name of the LORD be praised.

JOB 1:21 NIV

How do you praise God when you don't understand what's happening in your life and God is silent? You do what Job did.

Tell God exactly how you feel.
Focus on who God is—his unchanging nature.
Trust God to keep his promises.
Remember what God has already done for you.

_____

_____

_____

———— ✍ ————
When you feel
abandoned by God,
yet continue to
trust him in spite
of your feelings,
you worship God
in the deepest way.
———— ✍ ————

_____

_____

_____

_____

_____

_____

_____

_____

_____

*God, when I don't hear your voice or feel your presence, help me to
seek you, not a feeling. Then help me remember your promise that
you will never leave me nor forsake me.*

purpose #

2

YOU WERE FORMED
FOR GOD'S FAMILY

FORMED FOR GOD'S FAMILY

His unchanging plan has always been to adopt us into his own family by bringing us to himself through Jesus Christ.

EPHESIANS 1:5 NLT

POINT TO PONDER: I was formed for God's family.

QUESTION TO CONSIDER: How can I start treating other believers like members of my own family? What could I do today?

God wants a family, and he created you to be a part of it. This is God's second purpose for your life, which he planned before you were born. The entire Bible is the story of God building a family who will love him, honor him, and reign with him forever.

_____

_____

_____

_____

_____

_____

_____

_____

_____

_____

_____

_____

_____

_____

_____

FORMED FOR GOD'S FAMILY

The moment you were spiritually born into God's family, you were given some astounding birthday gifts: the family name, the family likeness, family privileges, family intimate access, and the family inheritance! As children in God's family we are given: *the riches ... of his grace ... kindness ... patience ... glory ... wisdom ... power ... and mercy* (Ephesians 1:7; Romans 2:4; 9:23; 11:33; Ephesians 3:16; 2:4). We also inherit eternal life. What an inheritance! You are far richer than you realize.

_____

_____

_____

_____

_____

_____

_____

_____

_____

_____

_____

_____

_____

_____

_____

_____

_____

——————— ✍ ———————

God has reserved a priceless inheritance for his children.
It is kept in heaven for you, pure and undefiled, beyond
the reach of change and decay.

1 PETER 1:4 NLT

_____ ✎ _____

Jesus and the people he makes holy all belong to
the same family. That is why he isn't ashamed
to call them his brothers and sisters.
HEBREWS 2:11 CEV

Because Jesus makes you holy, God is proud of you. Being included in
God's family is the highest honor, the greatest privilege you and I will ever
receive. Nothing else comes close. Why not pause right now and thank God
that he included you?

_____

_____

_____

_____

_____

_____

_____

_____

_____

_____

_____

_____

_____

_____

_____

*Thank you dear God, that you made me to be a part of your
family forever! What a privilege it is to be included. Help me to
never take your church for granted.*

WHAT MATTERS MOST

*The entire law is summed up in a single command:
"Love your neighbor as yourself."*

GALATIANS 5:14 NIV

POINT TO PONDER: Life is all about love.

QUESTION TO CONSIDER: Honestly, are relationships the top priority in my life? How could I insure that they are?

Since God is love, the most important lesson he wants you to learn on earth is how to love. It is in loving that we are most like him, so love is the foundation of every command he's given us. God wants us to love everyone, but he is particularly concerned that we learn to love others in his family. This is the second purpose of your life and it's called fellowship. Jesus said our love for each other is our greatest witness to the world.

_____

_____

_____

_____

_____

_____

_____

_____

_____

_____

_____

*No matter what I say, what I believe, and what I do,
I'm bankrupt without love.*
1 CORINTHIANS 13:3 MSG

The best use of your life is love. It should be your top priority, your primary objective, your greatest ambition. Love is not a good part of your life; it's *the most* important part. Relationships must have first place in your life above everything else. Why? God gives us three reasons: life without love is really worthless; love will last forever; and love is what you'll be evaluated on in eternity. Jesus summarized what matters most to God in two statements: love God and love people.

_____

_____
_____
_____
_____
_____
_____
_____
_____
_____
_____
_____
_____
_____
_____
_____
_____
_____
_____

Let love be your greatest aim.
1 CORINTHIANS 14:1 LB

———————— 〰 ————————

Our love should not be just words and talk; it must
be true love, which shows itself in action.
1 JOHN 3:18 TEV

The best expression of love is time. Time is your most precious gift because
you only have a set amount of it. You can make more money but you can't
make more time. When you give someone your time, you are giving them a
portion of your life that you'll never get back. Your time is your life. That's
why the greatest gift you can give someone is your time. Whenever you give
your time you're making a sacrifice, and sacrifice is the essence of love.

_____

_____

_____

_____

_____

_____

_____

_____

_____

_____

_____

_____

_____

Father, help me to remember that life is all about love.
Today I will take the time to love the people you place in my path.
Remind me that loving others is never a waste of time.
Teach me to love those who seem unlovable and give them
what they need, not what they deserve.

Whenever we have the opportunity we
should do good to everyone.
GALATIANS 6:10 NLT

The best time to love is now. You don't know how long you'll have the
opportunity to express love. Circumstances change. People die. Children
grow up. You have no guarantee of tomorrow. If you want to express love
you'd better do it now.

_____

_____

_____

_____

_____

_____

_____

_____

_____

_____

_____

_____

_____

_____

_____

_____

Father, help me to remember that life is all about love. Today I will
take the time to love the people you place in my path. Remind me
that loving others is never a waste of time. Teach me to love those who
seem unlovable and give them what they need, not what they deserve.

A PLACE TO BELONG

In Christ we who are many form one body, and each
member belongs to all the others.
ROMANS 12:5 NIV

POINT TO PONDER: I'm called to belong, not just believe.

QUESTION TO CONSIDER: Does my level of involvement in my church demonstrate that I love and am committed to God's family?

Even in the perfect, sinless environment of Eden God said, "It is not good for the man to be alone" (Genesis 2:18). We're created for community, fashioned for fellowship, formed for a family, and none of us can fulfill God's purposes by ourselves. While your relationship to Christ is personal, God never intends it to be private. In God's family you're connected to every other believer, and we'll belong to each other for eternity. *You are members of God's very own family, citizens of God's country, and you belong in God's household with every other Christian* (Ephesians 2:19 LB).

_____

_____

_____

_____

_____

_____

_____

_____

_____

_____

_____

To Paul, being a member of the church meant being a vital organ of a living body, an indispensable, interconnected part of the body of Christ. We need to recover and practice the biblical meaning of membership. The church is a body, not a building; an organism, not an organization. You were created for a specific role in Christ's body, but you'll miss this second purpose of your life if you're not attached to a living, local church. We discover our role in life through our relationships with others and significance comes, not from within yourself, but from being a part of Christ's body.

The local church is the classroom for learning how to get along in God's family. It is a lab for practicing love. Only in regular contact with ordinary, imperfect believers can we learn real fellowship, and experience the New Testament truth of being *connected* and *dependent* on each other. True fellowship is being as committed to each other as we are to Jesus Christ. And when we come together in love as a church family from different backgrounds, race, and social status it is a witness to the world.

_____

_____

_____

_____

_____

_____

_____

_____

_____

_____

_____

_____

_____

_____

_____

_____

_____

Your love for one another will prove to the world
that you are my disciples.
JOHN 13:35 NLT

You need a purpose to live for, people to live with, principles to live by, a profession to live out, and power to live on. God intends for his church to provide these. In fact, the five purposes of the church are identical to God's five purposes for your life. Worship helps you *focus on God;* fellowship helps you *face life's problems;* discipleship helps *fortify your faith;* ministry helps *find your talents;* evangelism helps *fulfill your mission.* There is nothing else on earth like the church!

_____

_____

_____

_____

_____

_____

_____

_____

_____

_____

_____

_____

_____

_____

_____

_____

Dear God, help me to remember that whenever I become
careless about fellowship with other believers, I'm moving
away from you. Forgive me for the times I've gotten detached
from your Body, the church. Help me to stay connected and
committed, and love your church the way you do.

EXPERIENCING LIFE TOGETHER

Share each other's troubles and problems, and in
this way obey the law of Christ.
GALATIANS 6:2 NLT

POINT TO PONDER: I need others in my life.

QUESTION TO CONSIDER: What one step could I take today to
connect with another believer at a more genuine, heart-to-heart level?

God intends for us to weave our lives together. The Bible calls this
fellowship. Fellowship is *experiencing life together*. That includes unselfish
loving, honest sharing, practical serving, sacrificial giving, sympathetic
comforting, and all the other *"one another"* commands found in the New
Testament. When it comes to fellowship size matters; *smaller is better*. Every
Christian needs to be involved in a small group within your church, whether
it is a home fellowship group, Sunday school class, or a small Bible study.
This is where real community takes place.

We experience authenticity in genuine fellowship. Fellowship is not superficial, surface-level interaction. It's genuine, sometimes gut-level sharing. It happens when people honestly share themselves—their thoughts, feeling, doubts, fears, strengths, and weaknesses. Of course, this is quite a risk, requiring both courage and humility. It means facing our fear of exposure, rejection, and being hurt again. Why would anyone take such a risk? Because it is the only way to grow spiritually.

_____

_____

_____

_____

_____

_____

_____

_____

_____

_____

_____

_____

_____

_____

_____

_____

_____

_____

Make this your common practice: Confess your sins
to each other and pray for each other so that you can
live together whole and healed.
JAMES 5:16 MSG

We experience mutuality and sympathy in genuine fellowship. Mutuality is the art of giving and receiving. It's depending on each other. Mutuality is the heart of fellowship: building reciprocal relationships, sharing responsibilities, and helping each other. Sympathy is understanding and affirming someone's feelings. It meets two fundamental human needs: the need to be understood and the need to have your feelings validated. Sympathy says, "I know what you're going through and what you feel is neither strange nor crazy." Sympathy is entering in and sharing the pain.

━━━━━━ ✍ ━━━━━━

How wonderful it is, how pleasant, for God's people
to live together in harmony!
PSALM 133:1 TEV

We experience mercy in genuine fellowship. It's a place of grace, where your mistakes aren't rubbed in but rubbed out. Fellowship and forgiveness go together. Because we're all imperfect, sinful people we hurt each other—sometimes intentionally and sometimes unintentionally. That means we need massive amounts of mercy and grace in order to live together. We need to offer it and receive it. Fellowship happens when mercy wins over justice.

_____

_____

_____

_____

_____

_____

_____

_____

_____

_____

_____

_____

_____

Father, I want you to use me to help build real fellowship in my church. Help me to be authentic with others and not wear a mask. Teach me to show sympathy to those who are hurting and offer mercy to those who have stumbled.

CULTIVATING COMMUNITY

❧

We understand what love is when we realize that
Christ gave his life for us. That means we must give
our lives for other believers.
1 JOHN 3:16 GWT

POINT TO PONDER: Community requires commitment.

QUESTION TO CONSIDER: How could I help cultivate the
characteristics of real community in my small group and church?

To help build genuine fellowship in your church or small group, you must
make the effort to do five things: be honest, be humble, be courteous,
respect confidentiality, and have frequent, regular contact with others.
Relationships take time and effort, but the benefits far outweigh the costs
and Jesus expects us to love each other the way he loves us.

_____

_____

_____

_____

_____

_____

_____

_____

_____

❧

You can develop a healthy, robust community that lives right with
God and enjoy its results only if you do the hard work of getting
along with each other, treating each other with dignity and honor.
JAMES 3:18 MSG

Make the effort to be humble and courteous. Humility is the oil that smoothes and soothes relationships. The Bible says in 1 Peter 5:5, *Clothe yourselves with humility toward one another, because God opposes the proud but gives grace to the humble.* Courtesy is showing respect for our differences, and being considerate even when we disagree with each other. Paul told Titus that there should be *"no insults, no fights. God's people should be bighearted and courteous."* We all have peculiar quirks and annoying traits. But community has nothing to do with compatibility. The basis for our fellowship is our relationship to God; we're family.

᠀

Let us not give up the habit of meeting together, as some
are doing. Instead, let us encourage one another.
HEBREWS 10:25 TEV

Deep fellowship is built with confidentiality. Only in the safe environment of
warm acceptance and trusted confidentiality will people open up and share
their deepest hurts, needs, and mistakes. Confidentiality means that what is
shared in your group needs to stay in your group. Also, deep fellowship is
built with frequency. You must have frequent, regular contact with your
group in order to build genuine fellowship with them. Fellowship requires
an investment of your time. Real fellowship takes effort.

_____

_____

_____

_____

_____

_____

_____

_____

_____

_____

_____

_____

_____

_____

_____

_____

God, help me not to settle for superficial relationships with other
believers. Help me connect to a small group of believers in my
church where I can learn what real love is all about.

RESTORING BROKEN FELLOWSHIP

❧

Do everything possible on your part to live in
peace with everybody.
ROMANS 12:18 TEV

POINT TO PONDER: Relationships are always worth restoring.

QUESTION TO CONSIDER: Who do I need to restore a broken
relationship with today?

Jesus said, "God blesses those who work for peace, for they will be called
the children of God" (Matthew 5:9 NLT). If you want God's blessing on
your life, and you want to be known as a child of God, you must learn to be
a peacemaker. Since you were formed to be a part of God's family and the
third purpose of your life on earth is to learn how to love and relate to
others, peacemaking is one of the most important skills you can develop.
*God has restored our relationship with him through Christ, and has given us
this ministry of restoring relationships* (2 Corinthians 5:18 GW).

_____

_____

_____

_____

_____

_____

_____

_____

_____

_____

_____

_____

_____

Peacemaking is not avoiding conflict. Jesus, the Prince of Peace, was never afraid of conflict. On occasion, he *provoked* it for the good of everyone. Sometimes we need to avoid conflict, sometimes we need to create it, and sometimes we need to resolve it. That's why we must pray for the Holy Spirit's continual guidance. Peacemaking is also not *appeasement*. Always giving in, acting like a doormat, and allowing others to always run over you is not what Jesus had in mind. Christ refused to back down on many issues, standing his ground in the face of evil opposition.

> As believers, God has called us to settle our
> relationships with each other.
> **2 CORINTHIANS 5:18** MSG

Here are seven biblical steps to restoring fellowship:

Talk to God before talking to the person.
Always take the initiative.
Sympathize with their feeling.
Confess my part of the conflict.
Attack the problem, not the person.
Cooperate as much as possible.
Emphasize reconciliation, not resolution.

RESTORING BROKEN FELLOWSHIP

Who do you need to contact as a result of this chapter? With whom do you need to restore fellowship? Don't delay another second. Pause right now and talk to God about that person. Then pick up the phone and begin the process. These seven steps are simple but they are not easy. It takes a lot of effort to restore a relationship. That's why Peter urged, *"Work hard at living in peace with others"* (1 Peter 3:11 NLT). But when you work for peace you're doing what God would do. That's why God calls peacemakers his children.

_____

_____

_____

_____

_____

_____

_____

_____

_____

_____

_____

_____

_____

_____

_____

_____

Father, give me clear vision to see how to best restore a broken
relationship. I need wisdom, humility, love, and courage to do the
right thing and take the first step to restoration.

day 21

PROTECTING YOUR CHURCH

❧

Let us concentrate on the things which make for
harmony and the growth of our fellowship together.
ROMANS 14:19 PH

POINT TO PONDER: It's my responsibility to protect the unity of my
church.

QUESTION TO CONSIDER: What am I personally doing to protect the
unity in my church family right now?

God loves unity. God desires us to experience *oneness* and harmony with each
other. The Trinity is unified and God wants us to be unified, too. Our heavenly
Father, like every parent, enjoys watching his children get along with each
other. Jesus, in his final moments before being arrested, prayed passionately for
our unity. And the Holy Spirit is the one who unites us in love.

_____

_____

_____

❧

The group of believers
were united in their
hearts and spirit . . .
In fact, they shared
everything.
ACTS 4:32 NCV

❧

PROTECTING YOUR CHURCH

Nothing is more valuable to God than his church. He paid the highest price for it, and it is worth protecting. Part of your responsibility as a believer is to protect the unity where you fellowship. You need to think of yourself as an agent of unity, commissioned by Jesus Christ to promote and preserve the fellowship among believers.

_____

_____

_____

_____

_____

_____

_____

_____

_____

_____

_____

_____

_____

_____

_____

_____

_____

_____

_____

Make every effort to keep the unity of the Spirit
through the bond of peace.
EPHESIANS 4:3 NIV

Here are some ways you can be an agent of unity:

Focus on what we share in common, not our differences.

Be realistic in your expectations.

Choose to encourage rather than criticize.

Refuse to listen to gossip.

Support your pastor and leaders.

Practice God's method for conflict resolution:

> *If a fellow believer hurts you, go and tell him—work it out between the two of you. If he listens, you've made a friend. If he won't listen, take one or two others along so that the presence of witnesses will keep things honest, and try again. If he still won't listen, tell the church* (Matthew 18:15–17 MSG).

_____

_____

_____

_____

_____

_____

_____

_____

_____

_____

_____

_____

_____

_____

_____

_____

---- 🖋 ----

Don't think only of your own good. Think of other
Christians and what is best for them.
1 CORINTHIANS 10:24 NLT

I challenge you to accept your responsibility to protect and promote the
unity of your church. Put your full effort into it and God will be pleased. It
will not always be easy. Sometimes you'll have to do what's best for the
body, not yourself, showing preference to others. That's one reason God
puts us in a church family—to learn unselfishness. In community we learn to
say "we" instead of "I," and "our" instead of "mine."

_____

_____

_____

_____

_____

_____

_____

_____

_____

_____

_____

_____

_____

_____

_____

Father, I need your wisdom to act in ways that protect the unity
of your church. Help me to squelch gossip and instead be an
encourager. I want to be a unifier, not a divider.

purpose # 3

YOU WERE CREATED TO
BECOME LIKE CHRIST

CREATED TO BECOME LIKE CHRIST

As the Spirit of the Lord works within us, we become more and more like him and reflect his glory even more.

2 CORINTHIANS 3:18 NLT

POINT TO PONDER: I was created to become like Christ.

QUESTION TO CONSIDER: In what area of my life do I need to ask for the Spirit's power to be like Christ today?

From the very beginning, God's plan has been to make you like his Son, Jesus. This is your destiny, and the third purpose of your life. What does the full image and likeness of God look like? It looks like Jesus Christ! On earth, God's ultimate goal for your life is not comfort, but Christlike character.

_____

_____

_____

_____

_____

_____

_____

_____

_____

_____

_____

*God knew what he was doing from the very beginning.
He decided from the outset to shape the lives of those who
love him along the same lines as the life of his Son. . . . We see
the original and intended shape of our lives there in him.*

ROMANS 8:29 MSG

Only the Holy Spirit has the supernatural power to make the changes God wants to make in our lives. This process is called *sanctification*. It's not a matter of trying really hard to be like Jesus, but trusting and listening to his Spirit, who lives inside us. However, the Holy Spirit releases his power the *moment* you take a step of faith. He waits for you to act first. God also uses his Word, his people, and circumstances to mold us. God's Word provides the truth we need to grow, God's people provide the support we need to grow, and circumstances provide the environment to practice Christlikeness.

_____

_____

_____

_____

_____

_____

_____

_____

_____

_____

_____

_____

_____

_____

_____

_____

_____

_____

_____

CREATED TO BECOME LIKE CHRIST

———— ℘ ————

When he comes we will be like him,
for we will see him as he really is.
1 JOHN 3:2 NLT

Becoming like Christ is a long, slow process of growth. Spiritual maturity is neither instant nor automatic; it is a gradual, progressive development that will take the rest of your life. Our transformation into Christlikeness will be completed when we get to heaven or when Jesus returns. When we are finally able to see Jesus perfectly, we'll become perfectly like him. Jesus wants to make us like himself before he takes us to heaven. This is our greatest privilege, our immediate responsibility, and our ultimate destiny.

_____

_____

_____

_____

_____

_____

_____

_____

_____

_____

_____

_____

_____

_____

Jesus, I want to learn to think like you, speak like you, feel what you feel, and act the way you would act. Please use your Words and your Spirit to make me like you.

HOW WE GROW

Let God transform you inwardly by a complete change
of your mind. Then you will be able to know the will of God—
what is good and is pleasing to him and is perfect.
ROMANS 12:2 TEV

POINT TO PONDER: It's never too late to start growing.

QUESTION TO CONSIDER: What is one area where I need to stop thinking my way and start thinking God's way?

Your heavenly Father's goal is for you to mature and develop the characteristics of Jesus Christ, living a life of love and humble service. Spiritual growth is not automatic. It takes an intentional commitment. You must *want* to grow, *decide* to grow, *make an effort* to grow, and *persist* in growing. Discipleship—the process of becoming like Christ—always begins with a decision.

_____

_____

_____

_____

_____

_____

_____

_____

_____

_____

_____

_____

_____

Once you decide to get serious about becoming like Christ, you must begin to act in new ways. You'll need to let go of some old routines, develop some new habits, and intentionally change the way you think.

There are two parts of spiritual growth: *"work out"* and *"work in."* The *"work out"* is your responsibility and the *"work in"* is God's role. Spiritual growth is a collaborative effort between you and the Holy Spirit.

_____

_____

_____

_____

_____

_____

_____

_____

_____

_____

_____

_____

_____

_____

_____

_____

_____

Continue to work out your salvation with fear and
trembling, for it is God who works in you to will and
to act according to his good purpose.
PHILIPPIANS 2:12–13 NIV

Let God transform you into a new person by
changing the way you think.
ROMANS 12:2 NLT

Your first step in spiritual growth is to start changing the way you think. The way you *think* determines the way you *feel*, and the way you feel influences the way you *act*. To be like Christ you must develop the mind of Christ. The New Testament calls this mental shift *"repentance,"* which in Greek literally means *"to change your mind."* To repent means to change the way you think—about God, yourself, sin, other people, life, your future, and everything else. You adopt Christ's outlook and perspective on life.

_____

_____

_____

_____

_____

_____

_____

_____

_____

_____

_____

_____

_____

_____

_____

_____

_____

———— 🪶 ————

When I became a man, I put childish ways behind me.
1 CORINTHIANS 13:11 NIV

There are two parts to thinking like Jesus. The first half of this mental shift is
to stop thinking *immature* thoughts, which are self-centered and self-seeking.
The second half is to start thinking *maturely,* which focuses on others, not
yourself. Thinking of others is the heart of Christlikeness, and the goal of
spiritual growth. This kind of thinking is unnatural, countercultural, and rare.
The only way we will learn to think this way is by filling our minds with the
Word of God.

_____

_____

_____

_____

_____

_____

_____

_____

_____

_____

_____

_____

_____

_____

Dear Father, I want to cooperate with your Spirit's work
in my life today. Help me to listen to your teachings and
develop my mind like Christ's.

TRANSFORMED BY TRUTH

day 24

❧

Jesus said, "If you continue in my word, then are
you my disciples indeed; and ye shall know the truth,
and the truth shall make you free."
JOHN 8:31–32 KJV

POINT TO PONDER: The truth transforms me.

QUESTION TO CONSIDER: What has God already told me to do in his
Word that I haven't started doing yet?

The Spirit of God uses the Word of God to make us like the Son of God. To
become like Jesus, we must fill our lives with his Word. God's Word is the
essential spiritual nourishment you *must* have to fulfill your purpose. The
Bible is called our milk, bread, solid food, and sweet dessert. This four-
course meal is the Sprit's menu for spiritual strength and growth. To be a
healthy disciple of Jesus, feeding on God's Word must be your first priority.
Jesus called it *"abiding."*

_____

_____

_____

_____

_____

_____

_____

_____

_____

❧

People need more than bread for their life;
they must feed on every word of God.
MATTHEW 4:4 NLT

Abiding in God's Word is a lifestyle that includes three daily decisions. First, I must accept its authority. The most important task you can do today is settle this issue of what's going to be the ultimate authority for your life. Decide that regardless of culture, tradition, reason, or emotion you choose the Bible as your final authority. Determine to first ask, "What does the Bible say?" when making decisions. Settle it in your mind that when God says to do something you'll trust God's Word and do it whether or not it makes sense, or if you feel like doing it.

Every word of God
is flawless.
PROVERBS 30:5

To abide in God's Word I must assimilate its truth. There are five ways to do this:

1. **Receive** God's Word—listen and accept it with an open, receptive attitude.
2. **Read** the Bible daily—it will keep you in range of God's voice.
3. **Research** or study the Bible, asking questions about the text and writing down your insights.
4. **Remember** it—memorizing Bible verses will help you resist temptation, make wise decisions, build confidence, offer good advice, and share your faith with others.
5. **Reflect** daily on Scripture—there is no other habit that can do more to make you more like Jesus.

_____

_____

_____

_____

_____

_____

_____

_____

_____

_____

_____

_____

_____

_____

_____

_____

_____

JB

Jesus said, "Now that you know these things,
you will be blessed if you do them."
JOHN 13:17 NIV

To abide in God's Word I must apply its principles. I must become *"a doer
of the Word"* (James 1:22 KJV). God's blessing comes from obeying the
truth, not just knowing it. The best way to become a "doer of the Word" is
to always write out an action step as a result of your reading or studying or
reflecting on God's Word. Develop the habit of writing down exactly what
you intend to do.

_____

_____

_____

_____

_____   ── *JB* ──

The Bible was not
_____   given to increase
our knowledge but
_____   to change our lives.
D. L. MOODY
_____   ── *JB* ──

_____

_____

_____

_____

_____

_____

_____

*Father, I thank you for your powerful, life-changing Word.
I want my mind to be saturated with Scripture. Help me
to build my life on your truth.*

TRANSFORMED BY TROUBLE

We know that in all things God works for the good of those who love him, who have been called according to his purpose.

ROMANS 8:28 NIV

POINT TO PONDER: There is a purpose behind every problem.

QUESTION TO CONSIDER: What problem in my life has caused the greatest growth in me?

God has a purpose behind every problem. You should expect four kinds of problems in life:

- **Trials** are designed by God to draw us closer to him and build our character. **Temptations** are designed by the Devil to draw us away from God and destroy our character.
- **Trespasses** are hurts caused by the sins of others.
- **Troubles** are usually, but not always, the consequences of our own sinful choices.

_____

_____

_____

_____

_____

_____

_____

_____

_____

_____

_____

_____

_____

_____

When you face a problem, try to determine the source first. If the trouble is your own fault, you should **repent** of it. If it is a temptation from Satan, you should **resist** it. If it is a trespass against you by others you need to **release** it through forgiveness. But if the problem is a trial from God, you need to **relax** and trust God in it. Regardless of the source, none of your problems could happen without God's permission. Everything that happens in the life of a child of God is *Father-filtered,* and he intends to use it for good.

_____

_____

_____

_____

_____

_____

_____

_____

_____

_____

_____

_____

_____

_____

_____

_____

_____

_____

For our light and momentary troubles are achieving for us an
eternal glory that far outweighs them all.
2 CORINTHIANS 4:17 NIV

Everything that God allows to happen in your life is permitted for one great, eternal purpose: to conform your character to the image of Christ. It is for your growth and God's glory, and it is a plan guaranteed to succeed. It will be completed when you get to heaven. The Bible says Jesus *"learned obedience through suffering"* (Heb 5:8 KJV). We grow the same way, and Jesus is our model. *We go through exactly what Christ goes through. If we go through the hard times with him, then we're certainly going to go through the good times with him* (Romans 8:17 MSG).

_____

_____

_____

_____

_____

_____

_____

_____

_____

_____

_____

_____

_____

_____

Dear God of all comfort, help me to remember that there is a
loving purpose behind every problem that you allow in my life.
Teach me to respond to the difficulties the way Jesus would.
Cultivate my character through the circumstances of life.
Help me to trust your purpose in my pain.

GROWING THROUGH TEMPTATION

God blesses the people who patiently endure testing.
Afterward they will receive the crown of life that God
has promised to those who love him.
JAMES 1:12 NLT

POINT TO PONDER: Every temptation is an opportunity to do good

QUESTION TO CONSIDER: What Christlike character quality could I develop by defeating the most common temptation I face?

To have the fruit of the Spirit is to be like Christ. How then does the Holy Spirit produce his fruit in your life? Instantly? No. Fruit matures and ripens *slowly.* God develops the fruit of the Spirit in your life by allowing you to experience circumstances where you're tempted to express the exact opposite quality! Character development always involves a choice, and temptation provides that opportunity. Every time you defeat a temptation, you become more like Jesus!

_____

_____

_____

_____

_____

_____

_____

_____

_____

_____

Overcoming temptation today

1. Refuse to be intimidated. Temptation is a sign that Satan hates you, not a sign of weakness or worldliness. It is also a normal part of being human and living in a fallen world. Don't be surprised or shocked or discouraged by it. Be realistic about the inevitability of temptation; you'll never be able to avoid it completely. The Bible says, *When* you're tempted ... not *if*. It is not a sin to be tempted. Jesus was tempted, yet he never sinned. It is not sin unless you give in to temptation, and that is a choice.

_____

_____

_____

_____

_____

_____

_____

_____

_____

_____

_____

_____

_____

_____

_____

_____

_____

_____

_____

2. Recognize your pattern of temptation and be prepared for it. There are certain situations that make you more vulnerable to temptation than others. These situations are unique to your weaknesses and you need to identify them because Satan surely knows them! He knows *exactly* what trips you up and he is constantly working to get you into those circumstances. You should identify your typical pattern of temptation and then prepare to avoid those situations as much as possible. The Bible tells us repeatedly to anticipate and be ready to face temptation. Paul wrote, *Don't give the Devil a chance* (*Ephesians 4:27 TEV*). Wise planning reduces temptation.

3. Request God's help. The Bible guarantees that our cry for help will be heard because Jesus is sympathetic to our struggle. He faced the same temptations we do. God's love is everlasting and his patience endures forever. If you have to cry out for God's help 200 times a day to defeat a particular temptation he'll still be eager to give mercy and grace.

When the Holy Spirit controls our lives, he will produce this kind of fruit in us: love, joy, peace, patience, kindness, goodness, faithfulness, gentleness, and self-control.
GALATIANS 5:22–23 NLT

_____

_____

_____

_____

_____

_____

_____

_____

_____

_____

_____

_____

_____

_____

Wonderful Father, thank you for the gift of choice. Help me to remember that temptation is always an opportunity to do the right thing. Today I choose your will for my life.

DEFEATING TEMPTATION

❧

God is faithful. He will keep the temptation from becoming so
strong that you can't stand up against it. When you are tempted,
he will show you a way out so that you will not give in to it.
1 CORINTHIANS 10:13 NLT

POINT TO PONDER: There's always a way out.

QUESTION TO CONSIDER: Who could I ask to be a spiritual partner to
help me defeat a persistent temptation by praying for me?

4. Refocus your attention on something else. Ignoring a temptation is far
more effective than fighting it. Once your mind is on something else, the
temptation loses its power. So when temptation calls you on the phone,
don't argue with it; just drop the receiver. To reduce temptation, keep your
mind occupied with God's Word and other good thoughts. You defeat bad
thoughts by thinking of something better. This is the principle of
replacement. You overcome evil with good.

5. Reveal your struggle to a godly friend or support group. If you're losing the battle against a persistent bad habit, an addiction, or a temptation, and you're stuck in a repeating cycle of *good intention-failure-guilt*, you will not get better on your own! You need the help of others. Some temptations are *only* overcome with the help of a partner who prays for you, encourages you, and holds you accountable. God's plan for your growth and freedom includes other Christians. Authentic, honest fellowship is the antidote to your lonely struggle against those sins that won't budge. God says it is the only way you're going to break free.

_____

_____

_____

_____

_____

_____

_____

_____

_____

_____

_____

_____

_____

_____

_____

_____

_____

_____

_____

6. Resist the Devil. Paul tells us to, *"Put on salvation as your helmet, and take the sword of the Spirit, which is the word of God"* (Ephesians 6:17 NLT). First, you must accept God's salvation. You won't be able to say no to the Devil unless you've said yes to Christ. Without Christ, we're defenseless against the Devil, but with *the helmet of salvation* our minds are protected by God. Second, you must use the Word of God as your weapon against Satan. Jesus modeled this when he was tempted in the wilderness. Every time Satan suggested a temptation, Jesus countered by quoting Scripture. There is power in God's Word.

7. Realize your vulnerability. God warns us to never get cocky and overconfident; that is the recipe for disaster. We must never let down our guard and think we're beyond temptation. Don't carelessly place yourself in tempting situations. Avoid them. Remember that it is easier to stay out of temptation than to get out of it. Every time you stand up to a temptation you become more like Jesus

———————— ❧ ————————

When people are tempted and still continue strong,
they should be happy. After they have proved their faith,
God will reward them with life forever.
James 1:12 NCV

_____

_____

_____

_____

_____

_____

_____

_____

_____

_____

_____

_____

_____

_____

Father, I need your grace in defeating the persistent temptations in my life. Give me the courage to share my struggle with a friend who can hold me accountable and give me support.

IT TAKES TIME

God began doing a good work in you, and I am sure he will
continue it until it is finished when Jesus Christ comes again.
PHILIPPIANS 1:6 NCV

POINT TO PONDER: There are no shortcuts to maturity.

QUESTION TO CONSIDER: In what area of my spiritual growth do I
need to be patient and persistent?

Spiritual growth, like physical growth, takes time. While we worry about
how fast we grow, God is concerned about *how strong* we grow. God views
our lives *from* and *for* eternity so he is never in a hurry. Discipleship is the
process of conforming to Christ. Christlikeness is the destination where
you'll eventually arrive, but your journey will last a lifetime. So far we've
seen that this journey involves *believing* (through worship), *belonging*
(through fellowship), and includes *becoming* (through discipleship). Every
day God wants you to become a little more like him.

_____

_____

_____

_____

_____

_____

_____

_____

_____

_____

_____

_____

Why does spiritual growth take so long? We are slow learners. We quickly forget God's lessons and revert to our old behavior. We have a lot to unlearn. The Bible calls this *"taking off the old self"* and *"putting on the new self."* We are afraid to humbly face the truth about ourselves. Only as God is allowed to shine the light of his truth on our faults can we begin to work on them. Growth is often painful and scary. Every change involves a loss of some kind. Habits take time to develop. Your habits define your character.

Everything on earth
has its own time and
its own season.
ECCLESIASTES 3:1 CEV

There's only one way to develop the habits of Christlike character: *practice* them over time! There are no *instant habits*. If you practice something over time, you get good at it. Repetition is the mother of character and skill. These character-building habits are often called *spiritual disciplines*.

_____

_____

_____

_____

_____

_____

_____

_____

_____

_____

_____

_____

_____

_____

_____

_____

_____

_____

———————— ✺ ————————

Practice these things. Devote your life to them so
that everyone can see your progress.
1 TIMOTHY 4:15 GWT

If it seems slow, do not despair, for these things
will surely come to pass. Just be patient! They will
not be overdue a single day!

HABAKKUK 2:3 LB

How to handle the wait: **Expect gradual improvement.** Believe God is
working in your life even when you don't feel it. **Keep a journal of lessons
learned.** Write down God's lessons so you can review and remember them.
Be patient with God and with yourself. God's timetable is rarely the same
as ours. **Don't get discouraged.** Remember how far you've come, not just
how far you have to go.

_____

_____

_____

_____

_____

_____

_____

_____

_____

_____

_____

_____

_____

_____

*Lord, when I get discouraged help me to see how far I've come, not
just how far I still have to go. Thank you that you will never give
up on me and will complete what you've started.*

purpose #

4

YOU WERE SHAPED
FOR SERVING GOD

ACCEPTING YOUR ASSIGNMENT

⟡

We are God's workmanship, created in Christ Jesus to do good
works, which God prepared in advance for us to do.

EPHESIANS 2:10 NIV

POINT TO PONDER: Service is not optional

QUESTION TO CONSIDER: What's holding me back from accepting
God's call to serve him?

You are here to make a difference by serving God and others. This is God's
fourth purpose for your life. Whenever you serve others, in any way, you are
actually serving God, and fulfilling one of his purposes for creating you. We
weren't placed on earth just to breathe, eat, take up space, and have fun.
God fashioned each of us to make a unique contribution with our lives.

_____

_____

_____

_____

_____

_____

_____

_____

_____

_____

_____

_____

_____

_____

_____

God redeemed you for the purpose of doing his holy work. You're not saved
by service but you are saved *for* service. In God's kingdom, you have a place,
a purpose, a role, and a function to fulfill. This gives your life great
significance and value. Once saved, God intends to use you for his goals.
God has a *ministry* for you in his body, and a *mission* for you in the world.

_____

_____

_____

_____

_____

_____

_____

_____

_____

_____

_____

_____

_____

_____

_____

_____

_____

_____

_____

It is he who saved us and chose us for his holy work not because
we deserved it but because that was his plan.
2 TIMOTHY 1:9 LB

———— 〰 ————

Jesus said, "Your attitude must be like my own, for I, the Messiah, did not come to be served, but to serve and to give my life."

MATTHEW 20:28 LB

For Christians, service is not optional, something to be tacked on to our schedules if we can spare the time. It is the heart of the Christian life. Jesus came to serve and to give—and those two verbs should define your life on earth, too. Serving and giving sum up God's fourth purpose for your life.

_____

_____

_____

_____

_____

_____

_____

_____

_____

_____

_____

_____

_____

_____

Wonderful God, help me remember today that I was put on earth to serve you by serving others. Thank you for the privilege of being a part of what you are doing through your church in the world.

SHAPED FOR SERVING GOD

God works through different people in different ways, but it is the same God who achieves his purposes through them all.

1 CORINTHIANS 12:6 PH

POINT TO PONDER: I was shaped for serving God.

QUESTION TO CONSIDER: In what way could I see myself passionately serving others and loving it?

You are God's hand crafted work of art. You are not an assembly-line product, mass produced without thought. You are a custom designed, one-of-a-kind, original masterpiece. God deliberately shaped and formed you to serve him in a way that makes your ministry unique. Not only did God shape you before your birth, he planned every day of your life to support his shaping process. This means nothing that happens in your life is insignificant. God uses *all of it* to mold you for your ministry to others, and shape you for your service to him.

_____

_____

_____

_____

_____

_____

_____

_____

_____

_____

_____

_____

How God Shapes You for Your Ministry

God never wastes anything. He would not give you abilities, interests, talents, gifts, personality, and life experiences unless he intended to use them for his glory. By identifying and understanding these factors you can discover God's will for your life. The Bible says you are *wonderfully complex*. You're a combination of many different factors. Five important factors form the acrostic "S.H.A.P.E." When God decided to create you, he determined exactly what you would need for your unique service. This custom combination of capabilities is called your Shape:

Spiritual gifts

Heart

Abilities

Personality

Experience

Spiritual gifts. God gives every believer spiritual gifts to be used in ministry. These are special God-empowered abilities for serving him. You can't earn your spiritual gifts. They are an expression of God's grace to you. Neither do you get to choose which gifts you'd like to have. God determines that. No single gift is given to everyone. Also no individual receives *all* the gifts. Your spiritual gifts were given for the benefit of others, just as other people were given gifts for your benefit. When we use our gifts together, we all benefit. This is why we're commanded to discover and develop our spiritual gifts.

Heart. The Bible uses the term "heart" to describe the bundle of desires, hopes, interests, ambitions, dreams, and affections that you have. Your heart represents the source of all your motivations—what you love to do and what you care about most. Your emotional heartbeat is the second key to understanding your shape for service. When you serve God from your heart, you serve with enthusiasm and effectiveness. Figure out what you love to do—that which God gave you a heart for—and then do it for his glory!

———————— ✦ ————————

We are God's workmanship, created in
Christ Jesus to do good works.
EPHESIANS 2:10 NIV

_____

_____

_____

_____

_____

_____

_____

_____

_____

_____

_____

God, you are an amazing Creator. Thank you for all your
attention to the details in my life. Thank you for shaping me to
serve you in a way that no one else can.

UNDERSTANDING YOUR SHAPE

—————— ❧ ——————

God has given each of you some special abilities;
be sure to use them to help each other, passing on to
others God's many kinds of blessings.

1 PETER 4:10 LB

POINT TO PONDER: Nobody else can be me.

QUESTION TO CONSIDER: What God given ability or personal experience could I offer to my church?

Abilities. Your abilities are the natural talents that you were born with. Some people have a natural ability with words. Other people have natural athletic abilities, excelling in physical coordination. Still others are good at mathematics or music or mechanics.

To apply your abilities in service, you need to understand four truths:

All of our abilities came from God.
Every ability can be used for God's glory.
What I'm able to do, God wants me to do.
If I don't use them, I'll lose them.

_____

_____

_____

_____

_____

_____

_____

_____

_____

_____

Personality. God created each of us with a unique combination of personality traits. God made *introverts* and *extroverts*. He made people who love *routine* and those who love *variety*. He made some people *thinkers* and others *feelers*. Some people work best when given an individual assignment, while others work better with a team. There is no right or wrong temperament for ministry. We need all kinds of personalities to balance the church and give it flavor.

_____

_____

_____

_____

_____

_____

_____

_____

_____

_____

_____

_____

_____

_____

_____

_____

———————— ❧ ————————

God works through different people in different ways, but it is the same God who achieves his purpose through them all.

1 CORINTHIANS 12:6 PH

Experiences. You have been shaped by your experiences in life, most of which were beyond your control. God allowed them for his purpose of molding you. In determining your shape for serving God there are at least six kinds of experiences you should examine from your past: *family* experiences, *educational* experiences, *vocational* experiences, *spiritual* experiences, *ministry* experiences, and *painful* experiences. It is this last category that God uses the most to prepare you for ministry. In fact, your *greatest* ministry will most likely come out of your greatest hurt. The very experiences that you have resented or regretted most in your life are the things God intends to use to help others!

_____

_____

_____

_____

_____

_____

_____

_____

_____

_____

_____

_____

_____

_____

_____

Gracious Father, I want you to use all the experiences that have shaped my life—both good and bad—for your glory. I am so grateful that you can even use the mistakes and failures of my life. Help me to help others the way you've helped me.

USING WHAT GOD GAVE YOU

Do your best to present yourself to God as one approved,
a workman who does not need to be ashamed and who
correctly handles the word of truth.

2 TIMOTHY 2:15 NIV

POINT TO PONDER: God deserves my best.

QUESTION TO CONSIDER: How could I make the best use of what
God has given me?

The best use of your life is to serve God out of your shape. To do this you
must discover, accept, enjoy, and develop the shape he's given you.

God wants you to discover your unique shape. Start finding out and
clarifying what God intends for you to be and do. First, assess your gifts and
abilities. Next, consider your heart and your personality. Third, examine
your experiences and extract the lessons you've learned.

_____

_____

_____

_____

_____

_____

_____

_____

_____

_____

_____

_____

_____

God wants you to accept your shape. Since God lovingly shaped you, and he knows what's best, you should gratefully accept the way he's fashioned you. Your shape was sovereignly determined by God for *his* purpose, so you shouldn't resent it or reject it. Instead you should celebrate the shape God has given only to you. Part of accepting your shape is recognizing your limitations. Nobody is good at everything and no one is called to be everything. We each have defined roles.

Since we find ourselves fashioned into all these excellently formed and marvelously functioning parts in Christ's body, let's just go ahead and be what we were made to be.

ROMANS 12:5 MSG

God wants you to enjoy your shape. Satan tries to rob our joy with two temptations that will prevent you from enjoying the shape God gave you: the temptation to *compare* your ministry to others, and the temptation to *conform* your ministry to the expectations of others. If you compare your shape, your ministry, or the results of your ministry with anyone else, you'll either get discouraged or you'll get full of pride. Either attitude will take you out of service and rob your job.

_____

_____

_____

_____

_____

_____

_____

_____

_____

_____

_____

_____

_____

_____

_____

_____

_____

_____

_____

———————— ✐ ————————

Be sure to do what you should, for then you will enjoy the
personal satisfaction of having done your work well.
GALATIANS 6:4 NLT

God wants you to develop your shape. God expects us to make the most of what he gives us. We are to cultivate our gifts and abilities, keep our hearts aflame, grow our character and personality, and broaden our experiences so we will be increasingly more effective in our service. Remember, you're going to serve God forever in eternity. Right now, you can prepare for that ministry by practicing here on earth. Never forget that we're getting ready for eternal responsibilities and rewards. This is why, like Olympic athletes, we keep training and developing.

> Kindle afresh the gift of
> God which is in you.
> **2 TIMOTHY 1:6** NASB

*Lord, you deserve my best. Help me to be creative
in making the most of what you've given me. I want
to spend my life serving you.*

HOW REAL SERVANTS ACT

If you give even a cup of cold water to one of the least of my followers, you will surely be rewarded.
MATTHEW 10:42 NLT

POINT TO PONDER: I serve God by serving others.

QUESTION TO CONSIDER: Real servants make themselves available to serve; pay attention to needs; do their best with what they have; do every task with equal dedication; and are faithful to the task they have been given. Which of the five characteristics of real servants is the most challenging for me?

While knowing your shape is important for serving God, having the heart of a servant is even more important. Real servants make themselves available to serve. A servant must always be standing by for duty. Being a servant means giving up the right to control your schedule, and allowing God to interrupt it whenever he needs to. Real servants pay attention to needs. They are always on the lookout for ways to help others. When they see a need, they seize the moment to meet it. *Since we find ourselves fashioned into all these excellently formed and marvelously functioning parts in Christ's body, let's just go ahead and be what we were made to be* (Romans 12:5 MSG).

_____

_____

_____

_____

_____

_____

_____

_____

_____

Real servants do the best they can with what they have. They don't make excuses, procrastinate, or wait for better circumstances. They just do what needs to be done. God expects you to serve him with whatever you have, wherever you are, right now. Real servants do every task with equal dedication. They follow the instructions found in Colossians 3:23, *Whatever you do, work at it with all your heart, as working for the Lord, not for men.*

Jesus specialized in menial tasks that everyone else tried to avoid. Nothing was *beneath* him because he came to serve. It wasn't *in spite of* his greatness that he did these things, but *because* of it, and he expects us to follow his example.

———————— ✍ ————————

Put on the apron of humility, to serve one another.
1 PETER 5:5 TEV

Real servants are faithful to their ministry. They finish their tasks, fulfill their responsibilities, keep their promises, and complete their commitments. They don't leave a job half done and they don't quit when they get discouraged. They are trustworthy and dependable. Real servants maintain a low profile. They don't promote or call attention to themselves. If recognized for their service, they humbly accept it, but don't allow notoriety to distract them from their work. Real servants don't serve for the approval or applause of others. They live for an audience of One.

_____

_____

_____

_____

_____

_____

_____

_____

_____

_____

_____

_____

_____

Jesus, today I make myself available to be used by you to serve others
in your name. I want to spend my life in serving you.

THINKING LIKE A SERVANT

Your attitude should be the same as that of Christ Jesus.
PHILIPPIANS 2:5 NIV

POINT TO PONDER: To be a servant I must think like a servant.

QUESTION TO CONSIDER: Am I usually more concerned about being served or finding ways to serve others?

To be a servant you must think like a servant. God is always more interested in *why* we do something than in what we do. Real servants are self-forgetful. They focus on others, not themselves. This is what it means to lose your life—forgetting yourself in service to others. Jesus *emptied himself by taking on the form of a servant* (Philippians 2:7 GW). You can't be a servant if you're full of yourself. It's only when we forget ourselves that we do the things that deserve to be remembered.

_____

_____

_____

_____

_____

_____

_____

_____

_____

_____

_____

_____

_____

Real servants think like stewards, not owners. They remember God owns it all. In the Bible, a steward was a servant entrusted to manage an estate. Servanthood and stewardship go together since God expects us to be trustworthy in both. The Bible says, *The one thing required of such servants is that they be faithful to their master* (1 Corinthians 4:2 TEV). Real servants think about their own responsibilities, not what other servants are doing. They don't compare, criticize, or compete with other servants or ministries. They're too busy doing the work God has given them. Real servants don't complain of unfairness, don't have pity-parties, and don't resent those not serving. They just trust God and keep serving.

Real servants base their identity in Christ. They remember they are unconditionally loved and accepted by grace so they don't have to prove their worth and they aren't threatened by lowly jobs. One of the most profound examples of serving from a secure self-image is Jesus washing the feet of his disciples. Real servants think of ministry as an opportunity, not an obligation. They enjoy helping people, meeting needs, and doing ministry. They *serve the LORD with gladness* (Psalm 100:2 KJV). God will use you if you'll begin to act and think like a servant.

_____

_____

_____

_____

_____

_____

_____

_____

_____

_____

_____

_____

_____

_____

Father, help me to do what I can, with what I have, for you today.
Help me not compare or compete with others who serve you. Help
me focus solely on what you've called me to do.

GOD'S POWER IN YOUR WEAKNESS

—— ✍ ——

Jesus said, "My grace is sufficient for you, for my
power is made perfect in weakness."
2 CORINTHIANS 12:9

POINT TO PONDER: God works best in weakness.

QUESTION TO CONSIDER: Am I limiting God's power in my life by
trying to hide my weaknesses? What do I need to be honest about in order
to help others?

God will use us if we allow him to work through our weaknesses. For that
to happen, we must follow the model of Paul:

Admit your weaknesses. Own up to your imperfections. Be honest about
yourself. There are two great confessions in the New Testament: The first
was Peter's, who said to Jesus, *"You are the Christ, the Son of the living God"*
(Matthew 16:16). The second was Paul's, who said to an idolizing crowd,
"We are only human beings like you" (Acts 14:15 NCV).

_____

_____

_____

_____

_____

_____

_____

_____

_____

_____

GOD'S POWER IN YOUR WEAKNESS

Be grateful for your weaknesses. Gratitude is an expression of faith in the goodness of God. It says, "God, I believe you love me, and know what's best for me." Paul gives us several reasons to be grateful for our inborn weaknesses. First, they cause us to depend on God. Our weaknesses also prevent arrogance. They encourage fellowship between believers. Most of all, our weaknesses increase our capacity for sympathy and ministry. God wants you to have a Christlike ministry on earth. That means other people are going to find healing in your wounds. Your greatest life messages and your most effective ministry will come out of your deepest hurts.

_____

_____

_____

_____

_____

_____

_____

_____

_____

_____

_____

_____

_____

_____

_____

_____

_____

_____

_____

GOD'S POWER IN YOUR WEAKNESS

Honestly share your weaknesses. Ministry begins with vulnerability. Paul openly shared his failures, his feelings, his frustrations, and his fears. Of course, when you open up your life to others, you risk rejection. But the benefits are worth the risk. Vulnerability is the pathway to intimacy. This is why God wants to use your weaknesses, not just your strengths. If all people see are your strengths, they get discouraged and think, "Well, good for her, but I'll never be able to do that." But when they see God using you in spite of your weaknesses, it encourages them to think, "Maybe God could use me!"

_____

_____

_____

_____

_____

_____

_____

_____

_____

_____

_____

_____

_____

_____

_____

———————— ✍ ————————

We are weak . . . yet by God's power we will
live with him to serve you.
2 CORINTHIANS 13:4 NIV

I am with you; that is all you need. My power
shows up best in weak people.
2 CORINTHIANS 12:9 LB

Glory in your weaknesses. Instead of posing as self-confident and invincible,
see yourself as a trophy of grace. When Satan points out your weaknesses,
agree with him and fill your heart with praise for Jesus who *understands
every weakness of ours* (Hebrews 4:14 CEV) and for the Holy Spirit who *helps
us in our weakness* (Romans 8:26). God is never limited by our limitations.

_____

_____

_____

_____

_____

_____

_____

_____

_____

_____

_____

_____

Father, use my weaknesses to show your glory.
Let my weaknesses cause me to depend on you completely.
Let my life be an example of what you can do through
ordinary people who are yielded to you.

purpose # 5

YOU WERE MADE FOR A MISSION

MADE FOR A MISSION

✦

Jesus said, "Go and make disciples of all nations, baptizing them in the name of the Father and of the Son and of the Holy Spirit, and teaching them to obey everything I have commanded you. And surely I am with you always, to the very end of the age."
MATTHEW 28:19–20 NIV

POINT TO PONDER: I was made for a mission.

QUESTION TO CONSIDER: What fears have kept me from fulfilling the mission God made me to accomplish? What keeps me from telling others the Good News?

Your mission—introducing people to God—is the fifth purpose of your life. There are a number of reasons why you need to take this mission seriously. **Jesus commands us to continue his mission.** The Great Commission was not given to pastors but to *every* follower of Jesus. You are the only Christian some people will ever know and your mission is to share Jesus with them. **Your mission is a great privilege.** Although it is a profound responsibility, it is also an incredible honor to be used by God.

_____

_____

_____

_____

_____

_____

_____

_____

_____

_____

Your mission is the greatest thing you can do for someone. We have the greatest news in the world and sharing it is the greatest kindness you can show to anyone. **Your mission has eternal significance.** Nothing else you do will ever matter as much as helping people establish an eternal relationship with God. **Your mission gives your life meaning.** If just one person will be in heaven because of you, your life cannot be considered a failure. **God's timetable for history's conclusion is connected to the completion of the commission we've been given.** Jesus will not return until everyone he wants to hear the Good News has heard it.

_____

_____

_____

_____

_____

_____

_____

_____

_____

_____

_____

_____

_____

_____

_____

_____

_____

_____

_____

_____

_____

_____

The most important thing is that I complete my mission,
the work that the Lord Jesus gave me.
ACTS 20:24 NCV

Completing your mission will bring glory to God. The night before he
was crucified Jesus reported to his Father, *"I have brought you glory on earth
by completing the work you gave me to do"* (John 17:4). Will you be able to
say that at the end of your life? **God blesses the life dedicated to his
kingdom.** The secret of being blessed by God is to participate in his agenda
for the world; to be a part of what he is accomplishing on earth.

_____

_____

_____

_____

_____

_____

_____

_____

_____

_____

_____

_____

*Father, thank you for the privilege of being a part of your plan for
the world. I want you to use me to bring others into your family for
eternity. Help me to reach even more people for Jesus.*

SHARING YOUR LIFE MESSAGE

Be ready at all times to answer anyone who asks you to explain the hope you have in you, but do it with gentleness and respect.

1 PETER 3:15–16 TEV

POINT TO PONDER: God wants to say something to the world through me.

QUESTION TO CONSIDER: As I reflect on my personal story, who would God want me to share it with?

There are four parts to the life message God has put within you: God wants you to share your testimony. The essence of witnessing is simply reporting your personal experiences with the Lord. In a courtroom, a witness isn't expected to argue the case, prove the truth, or press for a verdict; that is the job of attorneys. Witnesses just tell what happened to them. Jesus said, *"You will be my witnesses"* (Acts 1:8), not "You must be my attorney." *Those who believe in the Son of God have the testimony of God in them* (1 John 5:10 GW).

_____

_____

_____

_____

_____

_____

_____

_____

_____

_____

_____

God wants you to share your life lessons. The second part of your life message are the truths that God has taught you from experiences with him. These are *lessons* about God, relationships, problems, temptations, and other aspects of life. Write down the major life lessons you've learned so you can share them with others. We should be grateful Solomon did this because it gave us the books of Proverbs and Ecclesiastes, which are filled with practical lessons on living.

_____

_____

_____

_____

_____

_____

_____

_____

_____

_____

_____

_____

_____

_____

_____

_____

_____

———————— 〰 ————————

A warning given by an experienced person to someone willing to listen is more valuable than . . . jewelry made of the finest gold.

PROVERBS 25:12 TEV

God wants you to share your godly passions. God is a passionate God. He passionately *loves* some things and passionately *hates* other things. As you grow closer to him, he'll give you a passion for something he cares about deeply so you can be a spokesman for him in the world. It may be a passion about a problem, a purpose, a principle, or a group of people. Whatever it is, you'll feel compelled to speak up about it and do what you can to make a difference.

_____

_____

_____

_____

_____

_____

_____

_____

_____

_____

_____

_____

_____

_____

_____

_____

_____

_____

_____

_____

——————— ✍ ———————

A man's heart determines his speech.
MATTHEW 12:34 LB

———————— ✍ ————————

There is no fear in love; perfect love drives out all fear.
1 JOHN 4:18 TEV

God wants you to share the Good News. We must care about unbelievers because God does. Love leaves no choice. A parent will run into a burning building to save a child because their love for that child is greater than their fear. If you've been afraid to share the Good News with those around you, ask God to fill your heart with his love for them. As long as you know one person who doesn't know Christ, you must keep praying for them, serving them in love, and sharing the Good News. When you became a believer you also became God's messenger.

_____

_____

_____

_____

_____

_____

_____

_____

_____

_____

_____

_____

Lord, give me the courage to speak the unique Life Message you've given to me. Help me to break out of my comfort zone so you can speak through me. Put someone in my path today so that I can share your message.

BECOMING A WORLD-CLASS CHRISTIAN

ᔥ

Send us around the world with the news of your saving
power and your eternal plan for all mankind."
PSALM 67:2 LB

POINT TO PONDER: The Great Commission is my commission.

QUESTION TO CONSIDER: What steps could I take to prepare to go on
a short-term missions experience in the next year?

World-class Christians know they were saved to serve, and made for a
mission. They're eager to receive a personal assignment and excited about
the privilege of being used by God. Their joy, confidence, and enthusiasm is
contagious because they know they're making a difference.

_____

_____

_____

_____

_____

_____

_____

_____

_____

_____

_____

ᔥ

Jesus said to his followers, "Go everywhere in the world,
and tell the Good News to everyone."
MARK 16:15 NCV

How to Think Like a World-Class Christian

Shift from self-centered to other-centered thinking. This is a difficult mental shift because we're naturally self-absorbed. The only way we can make this paradigm switch is by a moment-by-moment dependence on God.

> Don't think only about your own affairs, but be interested in others, too.
>
> **PHILIPPIANS 2:4** NLT

Shift from local to global thinking. From the beginning God has wanted family members from every nation he created. The first way to start thinking globally is to begin praying for specific countries. Get a globe or map and pray for nations by name. Another way is to read and watch the news with *"Great Commission Eyes."* Wherever there is a change or conflict, you can be sure that God will use it to bring people to him. The best way is to just get up and go on a short-term mission project to another country! There's simply no substitute for hands-on, real-life experience in another culture.

_____

_____

_____

_____

_____

_____

_____

_____

_____

_____

_____

_____

_____

_____

_____

_____

_____

_____

Shift from temporal to eternal thinking. To make the most of your time on earth you must maintain an eternal perspective. This will keep you from focusing on minor issues and help you distinguish between what's urgent and what's ultimate. So much of what we waste our energy on will not matter even a year from now, much less for eternity. Don't trade your life for temporary things. What are you allowing to stand in the way of your mission? What's keeping you from being a world-class Christian? Whatever it is, let it go.

_____

_____

_____

_____

_____

_____

_____

_____

_____

_____

_____

_____

_____

_____

_____

_____

_____

Let us strip off anything that slows us down or holds us back.
HEBREWS 12:1 LB

Send us around the world with the news of your saving power
and your eternal plan for all mankind.
PSALM 67:2 LB

Shift from thinking of excuses to thinking of creative ways to fulfill your
commission. If you want to be like Jesus, you must care about what he cares
about most; you must have a heart for the whole world! You can't be
satisfied with just your family and friends coming to Christ. There are over
six billion people on earth and Jesus wants *all* his lost children found. The
Great Commission is *your* commission, and doing your part is the secret to
living a life of significance.

_____

_____

_____

_____

_____

_____

_____

_____

_____

_____

_____

_____

_____

*Father, I want to care about the whole world the way you do. Let
my heart be moved by the millions who have yet to hear the Good
News of your love. I accept the Great Commission as my
commission. Here I am, send me.*

BALANCING YOUR LIFE

_Live life with a due sense of responsibility, not as those who do not
know the meaning of life but as those who do._
EPHESIANS 5:15 PH

POINT TO PONDER: Blessed are the balanced.

QUESTION TO CONSIDER: Which of the four activities will I use to stay
on track and balance God's five purposes in my life?

Living with purpose takes balance and commitment. You can keep the five
purposes of your life balanced and on track with four simple activities:

Expression: Talk it through with a spiritual partner or small group.
The best way to _internalize_ the principles of purpose-driven living is to
discuss them with others in a small group setting. The Bible says, _As iron
sharpens iron, so people can improve each other_ (Proverbs 27:17 NCV). We
learn best in community. Talk through the implications and the applications
of each chapter.

_____

_____

_____

_____

_____

_____

_____

_____

_____

_____

_____

Evaluation: Give yourself a regular spiritual check-up. The best way to *balance* the five purposes in your life is to evaluate yourself regularly. God places a high value on the habit of self-evaluation. At least five times in Scripture we're told to test and examine our own spiritual health. To do this you need to regularly check the five vital signs of worship, fellowship, character growth, ministry, and mission.

_____

_____

_____

_____

_____

_____

_____

_____

_____

_____

_____

_____

_____

_____

_____

_____

_____

_____

_____

———————— ✍ ————————

Let's take a good look at the way we're living and
reorder our lives under God.
LAMENTATIONS 3:40 MSG

Reflection: Write down your progress in a journal. The best way to *reinforce* your progress in fulfilling God's purposes for your life is to keep a spiritual journal. Remember, this is not a diary of events, but a record of the life lessons you don't want to forget. We remember what we record. Writing helps clarify what God is doing in your life. Your life is a journey, and a journey deserves a journal. You owe it to future generations to preserve the testimony of how God helped you fulfill his purposes on earth. It is a witness that will continue to speak long after you're in heaven.

_____

_____

_____

_____

_____

_____

_____

_____

_____

_____

_____

_____

_____

_____

_____

_____

_____

_____

_____

_____

———— ✍ ————

Now I want you to tell these same things to followers who can be
trusted to tell others.
2 TIMOTHY 2:2 CEV

Replication: Pass on what you learn to others. The best way to learn
more is to pass on what you've already learned. Those who pass on insights
receive more from God. Now that you understand the purpose of life, it's
your responsibility to carry the message to others. You probably know
hundreds of people who do not know the purpose of life. Share these truths
with your children, friends, neighbors, and those you work with.

_____

_____

_____

———— ✍ ————
Passing on the
purpose of life is
more than an
obligation; it's one
of life's greatest
privileges. Who will
you share this
message with?
———— ✍ ————

*Jesus, now that I know your five purposes for my life, I ask
you to help me balance them. Don't let me overemphasize
one of them to the neglect of the others.*

LIVING WITH PURPOSE

❧

David ... served the purpose of God in his own generation...
ACTS 13:36 NASB

POINT TO PONDER: Living with purpose is the only way to *really* live.

QUESTION TO CONSIDER: When will I take the time to write down my answers to life's five great questions? When will I put my purpose on paper?

There are many *good* things you can do with your life, but God's purposes are the five essentials you *must* do. You should commit the rest of your life to doing them. Unfortunately, it's easy to get distracted and forget what matters most. This is why it is important to develop a purpose statement for your life, one that you can review regularly. A life purpose statement states the direction of your life, summarizes God's purposes for your life, defines success for you, expresses your shape, and clarifies your roles.

_____

_____

_____

_____

_____

_____

_____

_____

_____

_____

_____

_____

_____

_____

_____

_____

Life's Five Greatest Questions

What will be the center of my life? This is the question of worship. What are you going to build your life around? You can center your life around your career, your family, or many other good things, but none is strong enough to hold you together when life starts spinning apart. You need an unshakable center.

What will be the character of my life? This is the question of discipleship. What kind of person will you be? God is far more interested in what you *are* than what you *do*. Remember, you'll take your character into eternity, not your career.

_____

_____

_____

_____

_____

_____

_____

_____

_____

_____

_____

_____

_____

_____

_____

_____

_____

_____

What will be the contribution of my life? This is the question of service. Knowing what your combination of spiritual gifts, heart, abilities, personality, and experiences are, what would be your best role in the family of God? Is there a specific group in the body that I am shaped to serve?

What will be the communication of my life? This is the question of your mission to unbelievers. Your mission statement should include your commitment to share your testimony and the Good News with others, the life lessons and godly passions God has given you, and the special group of people God has appointed you to reach.

_____

_____

_____

_____

_____

_____

_____

_____

_____

_____

_____

_____

_____

_____

_____

_____

_____

_____

We beg you, please don't squander one bit of this
marvelous life God has given us.
2 CORINTHIANS 6:1 MSG

What will be the community of my life? This is the question of fellowship.
How will I demonstrate my commitment to other believers and my
connection to the family of God? Where will I practice the "one another"
commands with other Christians? To which church family will I be joined as
a functioning member? The more you grow in Christ, the more you'll love
his body and want to sacrifice for it. You can begin living a purpose-driven
life today.

_____

_____

_____

_____

_____

_____

_____

_____

_____

_____

_____

_____

_____

*Dear God, I commit the rest of my life to serving your purposes in
my generation —anywhere, anytime, anyway. Help me to spread
this message to others so they can become what you made them to be.*

————— 🖎 —————

Anyone who is joined to Christ is a new being;
the old is gone, the new has come.

2 CORINTHIANS 5:17 GNT

SOURCES

Text taken from *The Purpose-Driven Life* ®, Copyright © 2002 by Pastor Rick Warren. Grand Rapids, MI: Zondervan

Scripture taken from the NEW AMERICAN STANDARD BIBLE ®, Copyright © 1960,1962,1963,1968,1971,1972,1973,1975, 1977,1995 by The Lockman Foundation. Used by permission.

Scripture quotations are taken from the Holy Bible, New Living Translation, copyright © 1996. Used by permission of Tyndale House Publishers, Inc., Wheaton, Illinois 60189. All rights reserved.

Scripture taken from the Good News Bible in Today's English Version— Second Edition, Copyright © 1992 by American Bible Society. Used by Permission.

Scripture quotations are taken from the Holy Bible, The Living Translation, copyright © 1988. Used by permission of Tyndale House Publishers, Inc., Wheaton, Illinois 60189. All rights reserved.

Scriptures quoted from The Holy Bible, New Century Version, copyright © 1987, 1988, 1991 by Word Publishing, Dallas, Texas 75039. Used by permission.

Scripture taken from The Message. Copyright © by Eugene H. Peterson, 1993, 1994, 1995. Used by permission of NavPress Publishing Group.

Scripture taken from The New Jerusalem Bible. Copyright © Doubleday & Company, Inc., 1985, New York. Used by permission.

Scripture taken from *The New Testament in Modern English* by J. B. Phillips, 1958, New York: Macmillan

Scripture taken from *God's Word Translation* Grand Rapids: World Publishing, Inc. (1995)

ALSO BY RICK WARREN

Available from Zondervan

The Purpose-Driven® Life
The Purpose-Driven® Church
Planned for God's Pleasure
What on Earth Am I Here For?
Purpose-Driven® Life Scripture Keeper® Plus
Purpose-Driven® Life Video Curriculum
Doing Life Together – small group curriculum

Purpose-Driven® Youth Ministry
Purpose-Driven® Youth Ministry Training Kit
Doug Fields, youth pastor at Saddleback Church

Free resources available by writing:
free@purposedrivenlive.com

A subscription to the weekly Purpose-Driven® Life Email Devotional
Your First Steps for Spiritual Growth booklet
Personal daily Bible reading plan
How to pray for missionaries

For those in full-time ministry
Rick Warren's Ministry Toolbox, a weekly email newsletter for pastors
toolbox@pastors.com

If this journal has been helpful to you, we would love
to hear your story of what God has done in your life.
Send your story to Rick Warren at:
stories@purposedrivenlife.com